Voices From The West Midlands

Edited By Donna Samworth

First published in Great Britain in 2019 by:

Young Writers
Remus House
Coltsfoot Drive
Peterborough
PE2 9BF
Telephone: 01733 890066
Website: www.youngwriters.co.uk

Foreword

Dear Reader,

Are you ready to explore the wonderful delights of poetry?

Young Writers' *Poetry Patrol* gang set out to encourage
and ignite the imaginations of 5-7 year-olds as they
took their first steps into the magical world of poetry.
With **Riddling Rabbit, Acrostic Croc** and **Sensory Skunk**
on hand to help, children were invited to write an
acrostic, sense poem or riddle on any theme, from
people to places, animals to objects, food to seasons.
Poetry Patrol is also a great way to introduce children
to the use of poetic expression, including onomatopoeia
and similes, repetition and metaphors, acting as
stepping stones for their future poetic journey.

All of us here at Young Writers believe in the importance of
inspiring young children to produce creative writing, including
poetry, and we feel that seeing their own poem in print will
keep that creative spirit burning brightly and proudly.

We hope you enjoy reading this wonderful collection
as much as we enjoyed reading all the entries.

Contents

Finn O'Malley (7)	59
Rupert Joseph Cooke (5)	60
Jessica Durose (6)	61
Joshua Holmes (5)	62
Ed Collinge (5)	63
Jenson Daly (6)	64
Olivia Bowling (6)	65
Rose Keegan (6)	66
Poppy Ricketts (6)	67
Charlotte Young (5)	68
Amelie Page (7)	69
Joseph Carlson (5)	70
Liliana Tudor (6)	71
Phoebe Hateley (5)	72
Amelie-Rose Gilder (5)	73
Poppy-Lou Byng (6)	74
Nancy Newton (5)	75
Noah Mason-Byers (5)	76
Chloe Barrett (5)	77
Isabella Sault (5)	78

Regents Park Community Primary School, Birmingham

Safa Ahmed (7)	79
Uthmaan Dawood Badley (7)	80
Mohammed Jabril (6)	82
Abu Bakr Ahmed (6)	84
Ismail Raza (6)	85
Mohammed Isa Ahmed (7)	86
Aleena Begum (7)	87
Halimah Abdul Jalil (7)	88
Layan Basem (7)	89
Ali Jibraan (7)	90
Rayan Abdullahi (7)	91
Hajar Djeghroud (6)	92
Maryam Basem (6)	93
Taiyeba Chowdhury (7)	94
Leena Iman (6)	95
Hafsa Muse (7)	96
Raihan Ali (6)	97
Malaikah Iqbal (6)	98
Ibrahim Said Abdullahi (8)	99

RGS The Grange, Claines

Ruby Zishu Li (7)	100
Samuel Perry (6)	101
Harriet B (6)	102
Rosie Jane Bousfield (6)	103
Avni Wadhwani (6)	104

St Gerard's RC Primary School, Castle Vale

Julia Lachendro (6)	105
Noah Whelan (6)	106
Evan O'Toole (6)	107
James Lally (7)	108
Archie Foxall (6)	109
Ava Timmons (7)	110
Daisy Jay Dennis (7)	111
Ashlie Lambert (7)	112
Olivia Blenkiron (7)	113
Kian Teymoori (7)	114
Madison Spencer Ogiorumua (7)	115
Rose McCallion (7)	116
Peyton-Rose Franklin (7)	117
Violet Curtin (7)	118
Amelia Clarke (6)	119
Owen Christopher Mulligan (6)	120
Angel Payne (7)	121
Vivien Gondol (6)	122
Kyle Guest (6)	123
Mexxii Ryan (6)	124

St Mary's Catholic Primary School, Madeley

Daisy Taylor (5)	125
Leah Walker (5)	126
Rowan Simmons (6)	127
Hope Mapenzi Onyango (6)	128
Billy George Palmer (6)	129
Cerys Thomas (5)	130
Samuel Lloyd Carrington (5)	131
Reece Fellows (6)	132
Jan Samsom (5)	133

Harris Moorcroft (5)	134
Isaac Groom (5)	135
Blaine Fletcher-Cook (5)	136

Amal Sameed (6)	169
Eloise Hope (6)	170
Anna Housaini (7)	171
Shahan Hamzah Ashraf (6)	172

St Mary's CE Primary School, Shawbury

Omar Bilal Alfreahat (7)	137
James Ireland (7)	138
Noah Willoughby (6)	139
Evalyn Durie (6)	140
Peter Williams (6)	141
Harry Williams (6)	142
James Dale (7)	143
Isabelle Knight (7)	144
Harleigh May Jones (6)	145
Luukas Dean (6)	146
Alfie Titley (7)	147
Mollie Oakley (6)	148
Abigail Beckett (6)	149
Jake Hanson (6)	150
Joshua Poole (6)	151
Eva Marie Buckley (6)	152
Frayer Evans (6)	153
Ellie Giatsios (7)	154
Mia Edmonds (6)	155
Chloe Williams (7)	156
Jessica Butler (6)	157
Ethan Green (6)	158
Charlie Lowe (6)	159
Nahla Lewis (7)	160
Summer Williamson (6)	161

Tiverton Junior And Infant School, Selly Oak

Elle Lyza Marie Makinano Mananquil (7)	162
Shyanne Rahman (6)	163
Mohammed Kaif Ali (7)	164
Nirel Wangui Shitseswa (6)	165
Ryan Damdam (7)	166
Zaina Amrane (6)	167
Assiyah Rassam (7)	168

The Poems

Cool Daisies

C aterpillars climb daisies,
O n the green grass,
O n purple sites,
L ooking at frightening sights.

D amp leaves in the breeze,
A nd purple leaves,
I ncredibly shiny,
S ummer wave,
I s blowing and blowing,
E nd of winter,
S o that's the end.

Jay (6)
Bayton CE Primary School, Bayton

Unicorns

Unicorns smell like rainbow ice cream,
They look like shiny stars,
They sound like sparkling glitter
And dance beneath the stars.

They feel like clouds that are on the ground,
The beautiful creatures who make beautiful
sounds,
Their enchanting magical powers will
fascinate you for hours.

Zara Rose Bayliss (7)
Bayton CE Primary School, Bayton

Big Ben

B ig Ben, the famous clock,
I ts roof is a pyramid,
G inormous giant of the city.

B ell booms its chime every hour,
E veryone stares at the ninety-six-metre structure,
N ew in 1856, now being replaced and in London forever.

Monty Henry Hoare (6)

Bayton CE Primary School, Bayton

I Had A Little Dog And Its Name Was Scruff

I had a little dog
And its name was Scruff.
I sent him down the shop
For a penny's worth of stuff.
He dropped my box
And spilt my stuff.
I think my story is told
Well enough!

Kieran Carpenter (6)
Bayton CE Primary School, Bayton

Beautiful Beach

S ee the beautiful sea shimmering in the sun gracefully,

E at freezing ice cream as long as you want to,

A nd make big sandcastles with sparkly, shimmering shells.

Daisy Bayley (7)

Bayton CE Primary School, Bayton

The Coldest Season

Snow falls quickly to the ground,
it doesn't make a single sound.
Everyone's excited and rushes around,
every child makes screaming sounds.
Stomp! I tread on a twig,
it sounds very big.
People rush out to the skate on the frozen lake,
gliding carefully so that it doesn't break.
Icicles are shining bright like the sun,
children are having so much fun.
The wind blows wild around me,
snow falls quickly, it's all I can see.

Callen Chattertey (7)
Bellfield Infant School, Northfield

Winter

It's cold but bright,
It makes an extraordinary sight.
I don't know if it will snow,
Whilst in the house, the lights glow.
Snap!
The snow is too heavy for the trees,
When it snaps it sounds like a sneeze.
Snow falls like a flash,
It looks like a dash.
Icicles glittering in the sun,
While children eat a hot cross bun.
The children spend all day on the lake,
They are tired and their legs ache!

Freya Coombe (6)
Bellfield Infant School, Northfield

Winter Is Here

Snow falls gently to the ground,
And it doesn't make any sound.
Winter is here, and it's the best time of the year,
Children let out a cheer.
Snap!
The snow is too heavy for the trees
It sounds like a sneeze.
Snowflakes whirling and twirling,
While I pass by.
Icicles glitter in the sun,
While little children are having fun!

Fraser Henock (7)
Bellfield Infant School, Northfield

Winter

Snow falls gently to the ground,
it doesn't make a single sound.
I can see a light,
that shines so brightly.
Snap!
The snow is too heavy for the trees
when it snaps it sounds like a sneeze.
Children laugh and cheer,
because winter is the best time of the year.
The wind blows wildly around me,
the snow falls so quickly, it's all they can
see.

Jack Welch (7)
Bellfield Infant School, Northfield

Winter

All day long,
the snow goes strong.
People glide, side to side,
on the frozen lake.
Children cheer,
while grown-ups drink beer.
Up goes the fire,
while it is snowing,
People walk in slush and mush.
People skate while it is late.
In the sky,
thousands of stars are nearby.
In the coldest season,
people don't have a reason.

Eli McCorley-Sharpe (7)
Bellfield Infant School, Northfield

Winter Is Here

It's cold outside but it is a beautiful sight!
People skate on the frozen lake,
I think their legs are about to ache.
People stamp their feet,
it makes a really loud sound.
The sun shines brightly in the sky,
snowflakes whirl and twirl as they pass
nearby.
Snow falling quickly covers the trees with
snow.

Keyaan Khair (6)
Bellfield Infant School, Northfield

Winter Is The Best!

Snow falls gently to the ground,
and surrounds me all around.
Winter is here,
it's the best time of year.
Children play,
and let out a big cheer.
The snow is too heavy for the trees,
they snap and it sounds like a sneeze.
Children skate on the lake,
and they skate so much their legs ache.

Scarlett White (7)
Bellfield Infant School, Northfield

Winter

People run out to play on the frozen lake,
gliding carefully so it doesn't break.
Icicles shine bright in the sun,
people are having so much fun.
Snow falls quickly on this peaceful night
when we wake up it's a beautiful sight!
People skate on this frozen lake,
eating solid steak.

Larsen Fernandez (6)
Bellfield Infant School, Northfield

Winter Is Here

Winter is here,
it's the best time of year.
People rush out to skate on the frozen lake,
gliding carefully so it doesn't break.
Icicles sparkle brightly in the sun,
children outside having fun.
Sun falls quickly to the trees,
it's cold out here, can I go in, please?

Catrina Ali (7)
Bellfield Infant School, Northfield

Winter Is Coming Now

I'm surrounded by a thick, white blanket of
snow.
Snow falls to the ground,
and it doesn't make one little sound.
The children are playing,
very nicely twirling and swirling.
The wet snowflakes drop slowly to the
ground,
when I step on the ground, I hear a crunchy
sound.

Kara-Olivia Byrne (6)
Bellfield Infant School, Northfield

Winter Is Here

People skate on the ice,
and play nice.
The sun shines brightly in the sky,
snowflakes whirl and twirl as they pass me
by.
Winter is the best time of the year!
All around me, children spend their time on
the lake,
their legs begin to ache.

Georgia Kavanagh (6)
Bellfield Infant School, Northfield

Winter Is Here

All around me,
snow is falling quickly,
and doesn't make a sound.
Children make snowmen
and they smile.
People ice skate
and their legs ache.
Snow falls quickly on the trees
and my cheeks glow red when I play.

Jack Jon Jameson (6)
Bellfield Infant School, Northfield

Snowflake

Snow falls quickly to the ground,
and it never makes a sound.
The sun surrounds the Earth,
in all directions.
It is my favourite time of year,
Winter brings lots of cheer.
It is sunny,
it makes people funny.

Luka Fabian Dunne (6)
Bellfield Infant School, Northfield

Winter Is Here

I was in the snow,
I heard a beat,
it was my little feet.
The icicles shine,
while I have wine.
Snow falls,
by the walls,
Snow falls,
by the trees.
I have a big, big sneeze!

Maela Sheppard (6)
Bellfield Infant School, Northfield

Winter Poem

Snow falls quickly,
I don't hear a peep of sound.
I walk on my pond,
It doesn't break.
It is cold,
I can barely move my hands,
The trees are covered in snow!

Ryley Green (7)
Bellfield Infant School, Northfield

The Starfish In The Ocean

S ee the starfish under the sea,

T o see the beautiful starfish, you need to dive into the ocean,

A starfish is a very weird animal,

R ight at the bottom of the sea, you may see a starfish,

F ish and starfish live in the sea,

I and you may go under the sea,

S tarfish are the best animals in the world,

H ow would you think of yourself as a sea animal?

Anshi Mehta (6)

Hallfield School Pre Prep, Edgbaston

About A Stingray

S tingrays are very fast,
T urning and twisting on the sea floor,
I n the sea, it camouflages with the sand,
N ever touch a stingray,
G rey skin is my main colour.
R ay is not my name, I am a stingray,
A nimals hide when I swim by,
Y ou will find it hard to see me under the
sea.

Joobin Hariri (5)
Hallfield School Pre Prep, Edgbaston

Mermaid Magic Book

M ermaids love the sea,

E very animal likes mermaids because they are friendly,

R ipples on the surface show where we are,

M ermaids are special and a secret,

A t the bottom of the sea, the mermaid likes to swim under the water,

I slands are hot,

D own in the ocean they like to play.

Lucilla Murdocca (5)

Hallfield School Pre Prep, Edgbaston

Funny Dolphin

D olphins can swim underwater,

O n they go, to there and there,

L onely dolphins swim on their own,

P arty dolphins love each other,

H ome the dolphin goes,

I n the sea, dolphins can jump over the waves,

N ervous dolphins don't always go to see their friends.

Amelia Patel (5)
Hallfield School Pre Prep, Edgbaston

Dolphin In The Sea

D olphins have blowholes, every dolphin has a blowhole,

O ceans are playgrounds for dolphins,

L ong tail helps me swim fast along with boats,

P eople like to swim with me,

H elp me, people help me,

I help people,

N ice animals are dolphins.

Aariya Devi Sanghera (5)
Hallfield School Pre Prep, Edgbaston

The Stingray

S tingrays shoot splinters,
T he rays are very dangerous,
I n the sea, they eat big things,
N othing can eat the stingray,
G ills help them breathe,
R eally funny,
A ray is very fat,
Y oga, stingrays do not know.

James Barwell (6)
Hallfield School Pre Prep, Edgbaston

All About Seahorses

S eahorses live in the sea,

E veryone loves seahorses,

A ll seahorses are tiny,

H orses have the same head,

O ften in the sea,

R ed rocks, they swim there,

S ea is where they live,

E very day they swim.

Lamiya Kaderbhai (5)
Hallfield School Pre Prep, Edgbaston

Under The Big Blue Sea

O ctopus can eat fish,
C oco Pops aren't good for fish,
T op fish are blue,
O h, I love the ocean.
P op cans will make a shark die,
U nder the sea is blue,
S oap will go into the fishes eyes.

Hasan Nasar (6)
Hallfield School Pre Prep, Edgbaston

The Mermaid

M ermaids' tails are really shiny,
E very mermaid has a tail,
R eally shiny hair,
M ermaids are beautiful,
A nd mermaids eat seaweed,
I n the sea mermaids swim,
D own in the sea.

Thomas Balfour (5)

Hallfield School Pre Prep, Edgbaston

The Pufferfish

P ufferfish puff and puff,
U nder the ocean,
F ierce spikes come out when they puff,
F ish can swim under the water,
E ating seaweed and algae and other sea creatures,
R are and yellow.

Vincent Bartrum (5)
Hallfield School Pre Prep, Edgbaston

About A Snake

S nakes slither in the sea water,
N ever touch a sea snake,
A nimals fear me as I eat lots of them,
K inky wriggles and turning is my way to travel,
E ating fish is the nicest.

Aaraav Patel (5)
Hallfield School Pre Prep, Edgbaston

Sam The Crab

C rabs' claws make a clitter clatter sound,
R each with the long claws to touch the sand,
A nd on the bottom of the sea eat wet sand,
B eautiful crabs have pincers.

Henry Schaeferbarthold (6)
Hallfield School Pre Prep, Edgbaston

The Crab

C rabs' shells are enormous,
R ed-pink shells are crabs home,
A hard shell protects the crab's body,
B iting lots of fish and using their claws to catch them.

Zia-Kahn Hussain (6)

Hallfield School Pre Prep, Edgbaston

Scary Shark

S cary shark loves to eat fish,
H uge sharks have extremely sharp teeth,
A shark can eat meat,
R ats, the shark is going to eat fish!
K iller sharks.

Rohan Gangotra (5)
Hallfield School Pre Prep, Edgbaston

Sharks Getting Bigger

S harks eat animals,

H ard sharks are my fear,

A round the sea are sharks and some are bigger,

R acing around the ocean,

K ind sharks are not real.

Marcus Ngai (6)

Hallfield School Pre Prep, Edgbaston

Super Crab

C rabs can't fly, they are ginormous,
R ed pink shells protect the body of the
crab,
A crustacean is my real name,
B ubbles are under the sand.

Alexander Cooke (6)

Hallfield School Pre Prep, Edgbaston

A Mean Shark

S harks are strong and mean,
H ard and dangerous animals,
A shark has sharp teeth,
R acing around the sea,
K ing of the sea.

Ruben Singh Saini (5)
Hallfield School Pre Prep, Edgbaston

Shark Teeth

S hark is scary,
H ere is a shark in the sea,
A shark could eat anything,
R eal sharks are dangerous,
K ill people.

Hanson Liu (6)

Hallfield School Pre Prep, Edgbaston

Mean Sharks

S harks are scary,
H ave sharp teeth,
A shark's prey is a dolphin,
R acing around the sea,
K ing of the sea.

Ayansh Mathur (6)
Hallfield School Pre Prep, Edgbaston

About A Fish

F ish hide in the seaweed,
I t actually eats seaweed also,
S wimming and swimming in the sea,
H ere's a fish in the sea.

Mia Wang (5)
Hallfield School Pre Prep, Edgbaston

Crab

C rabs move zigzag sideways,
R ed crabs like hot places,
A crustacean is its real name,
B right sunlight scares it away.

Eshaan Sangha (6)
Hallfield School Pre Prep, Edgbaston

Slithering Eels

E els are electric, they are grey,
E els eat fish,
L ike to swim, eels have no fins,
S wimming about to electrocute.

Ibraheem Jawad (6)
Hallfield School Pre Prep, Edgbaston

Crabs

C rabs have claws,
R ed and orange is the colour of the shell,
A crab can't fly,
B ad crabs will bite people.

Joshua Theodore Emms (6)
Hallfield School Pre Prep, Edgbaston

The Orange Fish

F ish can swim in the deep blue sea,
I think that fish can swim,
S ome fish are dead,
H ot fish are hot.

Krish Kalia (5)

Hallfield School Pre Prep, Edgbaston

About Will The Shark

S hark bites,
H e lives in the water,
A big, brave shark,
R espect sharks,
K iller sharks.

Jai Vijh (5)
Hallfield School Pre Prep, Edgbaston

Under The Sea

A dolphin swims,
A dolphin swims with friends,
A dolphin eats fish,
Playing free with their friends.

Dhiya Paul (5)
Hallfield School Pre Prep, Edgbaston

Shark

Sharks eat fish,
Sharks have sharp teeth,
Rocks don't hurt sharks.

Ibraheem Abbas (5)
Hallfield School Pre Prep, Edgbaston

Shark

Sharks are great,
Sharks are not scary,
A shark lives in the sea.

Dhiryn Dubb (6)
Hallfield School Pre Prep, Edgbaston

The Magnificent Caterpillar

C rawls smoothly across the hard stone,

A rches her body like a rainbow,

T ickles my hand when she climbs up,

E ats her juicy green leaf,

R eaches a stem as tall as a giant,

P atterns on her smooth body camouflage,

I n and out of her plants in my garden,

L istening out for hungry birds,

L ater on, she wiggles her body like a worm,

A round her, she makes a beautiful cocoon,

R emoves her cocoon to be a magnificent butterfly!

Sophie Elvins (6)
Lickey End First School, Lickey End

My Little Pony

M y little pony is the best,
Y ou and me having lots of fun,

L et's play together all day long,
I like to brush your mane,
T o make it nice and straight,
T wilight Sparkle and your friends,
L eave me laughing with joy,
E very day is so much fun,

P laying games and telling jokes,
O nly stopping when it is bedtime,
N ight Mare comes to tell stories,
Y ou and I had lots of fun today!

Eloise Smith (7)
Lickey End First School, Lickey End

Seasons

Spring is all about a new start,
As animals give birth to their babies,
And leaves start to grow like a work of art.
In the summer the weather gets warm,
I love to play with my friends,
To dance and perform.
This is my favourite season, harvest and
Halloween,
I like to dress up in scary costumes,
And at school, we give donations like tins of
beans.
Winter is lots of fun,
With games, family and food,
Everyone is always in the best mood.

Grace Mason-Byers (7)
Lickey End First School, Lickey End

The Alicorn That Lost Her Magic

Emily the Alicorn had magic powers.
She could touch cold ice without her hooves hurting.
She could hear the hyenas, they were bad!
She gathered all of the animals so they didn't get hurt by the hyenas.
But the hyenas touched Emily and took all of her magical powers away.
Emily and her friends tried to look for the hyenas.
At last, they found them.
Emily spoke to the hyenas.
Her powers were returned!

Lauren Faulkner (5)
Lickey End First School, Lickey End

My Drone

I found a present under the tree,
The label said it was for me.
I tore open the paper and saw a box,
Was it a jumper, pants or some socks?
Was it a scooter or a proper phone?
"No!" I shouted, I always wanted a drone!
I took it outside and started to fly,
The drone went up high, high
And soon it flew above the houses,
Until I could see it no more,
"Dad!"

Charlie Maurice Levine (6)
Lickey End First School, Lickey End

Cheers To My Ears

Once upon a time, I had a test,
My hearing wasn't the best.
I needed to go to the hospital,
I met a man who was very tall.
He said to listen for the beep,
And don't you fall asleep.
I needed a hearing aid,
I had to wait for it to be made.
My hearing aids are peachy-pink,
They're really pretty don't you think?
I love my hearing aids.

Jemima Ford (6)
Lickey End First School, Lickey End

Summer Holidays

Summer holidays taste of fish and chips,
and ice cream for pudding,
Summer holidays smell like salty seawater,
Summer holidays sound like waves crashing
and seagulls calling,
Summer holidays look like children making
sandcastles and splashing in the sea,
Summer holidays feel like hot sun on your
face and sand between your toes,
Summer holidays are a real treat!

Isobel Langham (7)

Lickey End First School, Lickey End

Matilda

Matilda is a little dog,
Matilda likes to climb on logs,
Matilda likes to jump and play,
Matilda always gets her way,
Matilda is my special friend,
Matilda, I will love you until the end,
Matilda makes our house so fun,
Matilda and I can run, run, run,
Matilda gives the best cuddles,
Even when she jumps in puddles.
Matilda, I love you!

Harry Stockford (6)
Lickey End First School, Lickey End

Rabbits

R abbits love to eat carrots and lettuce,

A nd love to hop around,

B ouncing around and having fun,

B unnies are a nice pet to have,

I n the winter, some rabbit's fur turns white,

T he thick fur keeps them warm at night,

S nug and warm in their hutch, I love rabbits very much.

Olivia Roulston (5)

Lickey End First School, Lickey End

The Life Of A Penguin

P art black, part white,
E njoying gliding day and night,
N o flying for us,
G athering fish to eat,
U nder the white, snowy sky,
I ce, ice, ice, penguins love ice,
N aked penguins, we have no clothes,
S outhern Hemisphere is where you will
find us!

Freddie Mooney (6)

Lickey End First School, Lickey End

Football

F ootball is the best,

O n target to score,

O ffside!

T he ref called a red card,

B all is controlled by Grealish from

A ston Villa, my favourite team.

L ook how the skilful players score,

L ight on their feet as they win the game.

Finn O'Malley (7)
Lickey End First School, Lickey End

I Can't Wait To Try

S liding down the mountain,

N o rest,

O ff-piste,

W hite snow all around,

B ouncing on bottoms,

O ver hills,

A ir full of snow and wind,

R amps are super fun,

D angerous, but fun.

Rupert Joseph Cooke (5)

Lickey End First School, Lickey End

My Favourite Dance

I point my toes so they are nice and sharp,
I twirl here and there and all around,
I twist my body to touch the ground,
My skirt flows up as I jump in the air,
And of course, there is a bun in my hair,
Which dance am I?

Answer: Ballet.

Jessica Durose (6)
Lickey End First School, Lickey End

Crocodiles!

C rawling smoothly,
R eady and waiting,
O pen mouth slowly,
C reeping quietly,
O n the water side,
D eadly, sharp teeth,
I n its large mouth,
L ying in wait,
E veryone run! Aaaaahhh!

Joshua Holmes (5)
Lickey End First School, Lickey End

The Riddle Who Rhymes!

I can tell you how to make a cake, but I
cannot cook,
I can read a story, but I cannot hold a book,
I know every song, but I cannot sing a note,
I can teach you about the world, but I
haven't got a coat!
What am I?

Answer: Alexa.

Ed Collinge (5)
Lickey End First School, Lickey End

Spiders

Spiders are very hairy,
Some can be very scary,
Spiders lay lots of eggs,
When the babies hatch they have eight eggs,
Spiders make a web of silk,
Watch out, they might drop into your milk!
Spiders are great,
I have a spider as a mate.

Jenson Daly (6)
Lickey End First School, Lickey End

Our Friends In The Snow

I look like a bird,
I have wings but I can't fly,
I can swim,
I eat fish,
I live in the South Pole,
I like snow,
I cuddle my friends to keep warm,
I am black and white,
What am I?

Answer: A penguin.

Olivia Bowling (6)
Lickey End First School, Lickey End

Summertime

Summer feels like the sand on your toes,
Summer tastes like ice cream cones,
Summer looks like a sunny holiday,
Summer smells like barbeques every day,
Summer sounds like the ice cream van,
Summer really is a celebration.

Rose Keegan (6)
Lickey End First School, Lickey End

St Ives

I can see the sea crashing against the
shore,
I can hear the seagulls chasing me more
and more,
My bubblegum ice cream tastes delicious,
The Cornish pasties smell so good that I am
drawn,
I love feeling sunny and warm.

Poppy Ricketts (6)
Lickey End First School, Lickey End

Bertie Woofster

Bertie looks like brown freckles on a white wall,
His woof sounds like *ruff, ruff, ruff!*
He smells like soggy grass after the rain,
But he feels soft, like my favourite teddy bear,
Bertie is my best friend!

Charlotte Young (5)

Lickey End First School, Lickey End

Bigsby!

Bigsby, Bigsby, Bigsby,
Bark a song for me,
You bark for breakfast,
You bark for tea.
Bigsby, Bigsby, Bigsby,
Bark a song for me,
You bark when you see me,
You bark at everything you see Bigsby!

Amelie Page (7)
Lickey End First School, Lickey End

My Gorilla

G reat big monkey,
O ranges and bananas for tea,
R oars louder than a tiger,
I nsects for breakfast,
L ots of black fur,
L ong, sharp teeth,
A ngry and loud.

Joseph Carlson (5)
Lickey End First School, Lickey End

Penguins

The Daddy Penguins waddle,
Around their babies in a huddle,
While Mummy goes to get some fish,
To feed them all their favourite dish.
Black and white with orange toes,
And a cute beak for a nose.

Liliana Tudor (6)
Lickey End First School, Lickey End

My Turtle, Squirt

T hey are born on a beach,
U ntil they crawl back,
R eturn to their mummy,
T o swim to the sea,
L ike a tortoise on land,
E ats plants and have a shell.

Phoebe Hateley (5)
Lickey End First School, Lickey End

Swimming Lessons

My swimming pool is blue like the sky,
When I jump it goes *splish splash!*
The water smells clean and tastes of
chlorine,
And sometimes I choke on it,
My pool is sometimes cold.

Amelie-Rose Gilder (5)
Lickey End First School, Lickey End

Molly The Dog

M olly is my dog,

O h no, she's got my slipper,

L icks, kisses and slobber,

L ove when she sits on my lap,

Y ou're my dog, Molly, and I love you.

Poppy-Lou Byng (6)
Lickey End First School, Lickey End

The Sea

The salty sea on the cool, sandy bed,
The sea air blowing around my head,
Smells like mermaid's breath,
It feels like this is the only place in the world.

Nancy Newton (5)
Lickey End First School, Lickey End

About Lions

L ion, the king of the jungle,
I t hunts in long, wavy grass,
O range sun warms the lion,
N airobi, the lion's home.

Noah Mason-Byers (5)
Lickey End First School, Lickey End

I Make You Smile

I visit once a year,
I am furry,
I hop about,
I have big ears,
I bring eggs with sweets in.
Who am I?

Chloe Barrett (5)
Lickey End First School, Lickey End

School

S uper,

C ool,

H appy,

O n time,

O utdoor play,

L earning.

Isabella Sault (5)
Lickey End First School, Lickey End

PAW Patrol - One Shot

It was another wonderful day,
In the town of Adventure Bay.
Ryder received a call, and answered right away,
It was Mayor Goodway!
"Ryder, Ryder!" her voice was fizzing,
"Just be quiet and try to listen!"
Ryder listened and heard no sound,
He awkwardly shrugged and looked at the ground,
"You hear no sound when you listen,
Because someone came and stole my chicken!"
"Somebody help me!" The mayor yelped,
"Great!" said Ryder. "We're gonna help!"
He went to the lookout and called his pups,
And Marshall ran to the lift and tripped on some cups.

Safa Ahmed (7)

Regents Park Community Primary School, Birmingham

The Rescue

"There is a big splodgy mark on the seat of
my car,
You've gone too far!
I need to go and scream in the park!"

My mum sounded so loud, it shook the sun
and clouds,
"Today I don't feel very proud," she sighed
aloud.
Then the cat raced past me, meowed.
"Don't let her out, she is not allowed!"

Me and my brother eagerly ran out, to the
park and by the tree,
my mum shouts, "The cats on the tree
clinging on, help her out!"

We scramble up the tree,
And both did certainly agree,

To rescue the cat and apologise to Mummy
with a happy cup of tea!

Uthmaan Dawood Badley (7)

Regents Park Community Primary School,
Birmingham

Poem Of The Months

January is a New Year and a new beginning,
February is love and friendship,
March is when winter ends and spring
comes,
April is about bunnies and colourful Easter
eggs,
May is very colourful, with beautiful flowers
growing,
June is a warm breeze and wasps flying,
July is very hot and relaxing on the beach in
the sunshine,
August is a very long holiday break when
kids have fun,
September is back to school and autumn
starts,
October is when leaves fall and summer
ends,

November is when people see beautiful fireworks,
December is full of light, everything is white and the year ends.

Mohammed Jabril (6)

Regents Park Community Primary School, Birmingham

Baby Sister

B eautiful brown eyes,
A mazing acrobatics as she rolls around,
B ouncing up and down on Daddy's knee,
Y elling with delight.

S weet little sister,
I nside your crib, you go,
S leep silently, snuggly and warm,
T ravelling to your dreamland,
E njoy your restful sleep,
R emember always that I love you.

Abu Bakr Ahmed (6)

Regents Park Community Primary School,
Birmingham

Football Is My Favourite

F riends can always come and play with me,

O n the football pitch, I am very happy,

O ne-nil, we win,

T he other team sat next to the bin,

B rilliant times I have had,

A long with my best friend Fuad,

L osing at football, I'm not good at that,

L oving football, my kind of thing.

Ismail Raza (6)

Regents Park Community Primary School, Birmingham

Fierce Mom

T earing, hungry predator, hungry all the time,

I ncredible stripes on their soft fur, showing power not so weak,

G athering meat every hour and day with a set of teeth as sharp as a Samurai sword,

E ating slower than they kill, licking their mouth, basking in the sun,

R oar of a lion and beauty like my mum!

Mohammed Isa Ahmed (7)
Regents Park Community Primary School, Birmingham

Our Heroes

R emember the people that died,
E veryone should thank them,
M ost of them had families,
E ven small children,
M ay God rest their souls,
B ecause they are our heroes,
E very November on the 11th day,
R emember those who are not here today
(Amen).

Aleena Begum (7)

Regents Park Community Primary School,
Birmingham

The Animal Poem

I like to go on walks,
I do an important job every day,
Taking care of my owners,
In the garden, I love to play,
I have sharp razor teeth,
I have seven people to take care of me,
My eyes are orange like the burning hot ball
of sun,
Who am I?

Answer: My dog, Allen.

Halimah Abdul Jalil (7)
Regents Park Community Primary School,
Birmingham

Home

Home looks like sister's beautiful drawings,
Home sounds like Dad shouting, "Goal!"
Home smells like Aunty's yummy cookies,
Home feels like Nana's warm hugs,
Home tastes like Mum's delicious food,
Home is one big, loving family.

Layan Basem (7)
Regents Park Community Primary School,
Birmingham

Different Types Of Weather

Cold as ice,
Hot as the sun,
Mix it together!
Makes a beautiful, purplish sunset.

The wind is blowing,
Far away!

The rain is coming,
Falling out of the sky,
Wetting everybody.
Don't forget your umbrella!

Ali Jibraan (7)
Regents Park Community Primary School,
Birmingham

Rudolph The Red-Nosed Reindeer

I have a glowing red nose,
I am a magical pet,
I live in the North Pole,
I only travel the world on Christmas Eve,
My owner is Santa,
I have an important job,
Who am I?

Answer: Rudolph the red-nosed reindeer.

Rayan Abdullahi (7)

Regents Park Community Primary School,
Birmingham

Summer!

S un shining like a star,
U mbrellas locked in the cupboard,
M elted ice cream on my hand,
M y favourite time of the year,
E njoying the long days in the park,
R ainbows welcomed in the sky.

Hajar Djeghroud (6)

Regents Park Community Primary School,
Birmingham

A Time Of Year

The grey clouds go and the sun comes out.
My sky is blue,
You can go to the beach and sunbathe,
You can have some ice lollies to cool you
down,
In the garden, you can have barbecues,
I am the hottest season,
What am I?

Maryam Basem (6)

Regents Park Community Primary School,
Birmingham

Stars Shining

Stars shine bright like the sun,
Stars glow as bright as a diamond,
Stars sound like twinkling and shimmering glitter,
Stars make me feel enjoyable and confident,
Stars feel hot like balls of gas,
Stars are really shimmery.

Taiyeba Chowdhury (7)
Regents Park Community Primary School, Birmingham

The Nature Of Bunnies

B unnies hopping all about and
everywhere,
U nderground digging very long tunnels,
N ibbling on orange, delicious carrots,
N ot eating anything but carrots,
Y ummy carrots taste good to bunnies.

Leena Iman (6)

Regents Park Community Primary School,
Birmingham

Good Person

I like to help people,
I like to listen to my teacher,
I like to respect my elders,
I like to be friendly,
I like to be determined,
I like to achieve my goals,
What am I?

Answer: A good person.

Hafsa Muse (7)

Regents Park Community Primary School,
Birmingham

Family

F amily is my life,
A lways ready to help,
M y family is great,
I love my family,
L aughter and joy,
Y ummy cooking!

Raihan Ali (6)

Regents Park Community Primary School,
Birmingham

A Magical Creature

I am small,
I have wings,
I can fly,
I am magical,
I have a wand,
I love shiny things,
What am I?

Answer: A fairy.

Malaikah Iqbal (6)
Regents Park Community Primary School,
Birmingham

Riddle

I have nine eyes
I have two legs,
I am black and round,
What am I?

Ibrahim Said Abdullahi (8)
Regents Park Community Primary School,
Birmingham

What Am I?

I am cute and I have two colours,
I rolled down a hill and you can see black
and white,
I like eating bamboo,
I climb bamboo,
I live in Asia,
What am I?

Answer: A panda.

Ruby Zishu Li (7)
RGS The Grange, Claines

In The Incredible Sea

It lives in the ocean,
It can move at an incredible speed,
It is black and white,
It eats sea lions,
It lives near the shore,
What is it?

Answer: A killer whale.

Samuel Perry (6)
RGS The Grange, Claines

In The Jungle Of Magic

I'm glittery,
I'm magical,
You still can't guess?
Okay, I'll give you another clue!
I'm colourful.
What am I?

Answer: A unicorn.

Harriet B (6)
RGS The Grange, Claines

Guess What I Am

It has black and white fur,
It has a good sense of smell,
It has a long tail,
It can bark loudly,
What is it?

Answer: A dog.

Rosie Jane Bousfield (6)
RGS The Grange, Claines

In The Times Of The Magical Forest

It has rainbow hair,
It has a horn,
Can you guess what it is?

Answer: A unicorn.

Avni Wadhwani (6)
RGS The Grange, Claines

Snowflakes Fall Down

S un is gone and winter is back and it is
frosty,

N o more spring, now put on some warm
clothes,

O ut we go to the snow,

W e are cold, we are freezing now,

F rost in the freezing playground,

L ast winter was colder,

A nd try to escape from the snow because
it is freezing,

K ids come to play,

E verywhere is cold,

S now is cold, don't go out without your
warm clothes.

Julia Lachendro (6)

St Gerard's RC Primary School, Castle Vale

The Hailing Day

H ard, cold hail, banging loud on the window panes, shouting, "That is loud!"
A s icy, frosty, snowy wet globes hit the windowpane,
I ce is frosty, ice falls like meteorites,
L ittle frosty balls fall like little snowballs,
I ce like a meteor shooting from the sky,
N ow it is snowing like a fast tornado,
G round is covered in snowflakes and snowing icy icebergs.

Noah Whelan (6)
St Gerard's RC Primary School, Castle Vale

Snow Melting

S lippery snow makes people fall,

N oisy, chattering children play in the snow,

O n white, thick snow, excited children ride sledges,

W intery, cold, soggy snow is really cold like an ice cube,

I cy snow melts slowly in the warm, winter sun,

N early all of the thin, layered snow has disappeared,

G racefully, the wintertime stops and the snow melts.

Evan O'Toole (6)

St Gerard's RC Primary School, Castle Vale

Raindrop

R ain, dripping wet everywhere,

A ir dropping, rain dropping, like a rusty metal shower,

I cy, dripping wet wind everywhere, freezing cold wind blowing, water spreading,

N umb people everywhere.

I cy, freezing cold, dripping wet, slippy,

N umb, frozen purple toes, watery, slippery,

G rowling people shouting, "There's so much rain!"

James Lally (7)
St Gerard's RC Primary School, Castle Vale

Winter

I can smell winter like the wind,
I can hear wind whooshing,
I can taste winter like fish dinners,
I can feel my fingers freezing,
Snow is fun, snow is cold,
Ice is cold, ice is freezing,
I can feel snow like winter,
I can taste winter like hot chocolate,
Snow looks like ice cream,
I can see marshmallows falling from the sky,
Snow feels like cold ice.

Archie Foxall (6)
St Gerard's RC Primary School, Castle Vale

Winter Sense Poem

Winter looks like paper covering the wet,
soggy ground,
Winter smells like cookies baking,
Winter feels like ice-cold sun,
Winter sounds like children playing,
Winter tastes like hot chocolate,
Winter is like excited children in the snowy,
ice-cold sun,
Winter is really cold for children,
Winter is snowing slowly

Ava Timmons (7)

St Gerard's RC Primary School, Castle Vale

Summer Poem

S ummer is hot as fire,

U mbrella is burned by the big sun,

M assive, big, burned fire is as warm as the sun,

M assive, big, yellow sun is like fire, hot in the houses,

E very day it is sunny and hot like a house on fire,

R unning around the garden with the sun rising high.

Daisy Jay Dennis (7)

St Gerard's RC Primary School, Castle Vale

Winter Snow

Snow looks like white ice cream,
Winter is my favourite season because of
the snow,
The snow looks like marshmallows when
falling from the sky,
When the snow falls from the sky, it looks
like white cotton wool,
When I lick the snow it tastes like hot
chocolate,
The snow feels like white ice.

Ashlie Lambert (7)
St Gerard's RC Primary School, Castle Vale

Snowflakes

Snowflakes look like small, white stars falling,
Snowflakes sound like silent rain dripping,
Snowflakes smell like sweet-smelling snow dripping,
Snowflakes feel like freezing cold diamonds slipping,
Snowflakes taste like delicious cold ice creams,
Snowflakes really are the best.

Olivia Blenkiron (7)

St Gerard's RC Primary School, Castle Vale

High Hailing

Hopping high like a kangaroo,
Asking to come into a large mansion,
I'd love to come into a big, white mansion,
Like a big, white ice cream,
I see it bouncing on the floor,
Now the hail has stopped failing,
Going home, hail covering the ground like a blanket.

Kian Teymoori (7)
St Gerard's RC Primary School, Castle Vale

The Snow Poem

Snow looks like a pristine, tiny penguin,
Snow sounds like children cheering,
Snow smells like carrots for the reindeer,
Snow feels like freezing fingers,
Snow tastes like something cold on your
tongue,
Snow is fun but freezing indeed.

Madison Spencer Ogiorumua (7)
St Gerard's RC Primary School, Castle Vale

A Winter Poem

I can smell bubbling hot chocolate,
I can taste melting marshmallows,
I can feel my fingers tingling and shaking,
I can see the fluffy snow twirling onto the
soggy ground,
I can hear the white falling down to the
ground.

Rose McCallion (7)

St Gerard's RC Primary School, Castle Vale

Snow Is Everywhere

S now is as white as paper, dropping from the sky,

N ext, we will have snow everywhere,

O h, flakes nice and white and clouds flying high in the sky,

W inter is cold but snow is soft to play in.

Peyton-Rose Franklin (7)

St Gerard's RC Primary School, Castle Vale

Sunshine

Sunshine looks like a bright star,
Sunshine smells like a pretty, sweet flower,
Sunshine tastes of fresh, green grass,
Sunshine feels like a hot potato,
Sunshine sounds like the tune of an ice
cream van.

Violet Curtin (7)
St Gerard's RC Primary School, Castle Vale

The Frosty Day

When it is frosty, it feels calm,
When it is frosty, it tastes icy,
When it is frosty, it looks not busy but silent,
When it is frosty, it smells plain,
When it is frosty, it sounds of nothing.

Amelia Clarke (6)
St Gerard's RC Primary School, Castle Vale

Christmas Days At Winter

W intry snowflakes falling,

 I am in bed, watching through the icy window,

N o one at school,

T oes cold,

E ating warm snacks,

R aining down slowly.

Owen Christopher Mulligan (6)
St Gerard's RC Primary School, Castle Vale

A Sunshine Poem

Lovely, warm flowers in the lovely, warm breeze,
Icy-cold Coca-Cola drinking in the sun,
I see some beautiful, patterned butterflies,
I can hear some kids talking and playing.

Angel Payne (7)
St Gerard's RC Primary School, Castle Vale

Frost

Frost tastes like powdery icing,
Frost feels like freezing ice,
Frost looks like rough salt,
Frost smells like sweet icing,
Frost sounds like silence.

Vivien Gondol (6)

St Gerard's RC Primary School, Castle Vale

Hail

Hail looks like rocks,
Hail sounds like some rattlesnakes,
Hail smells like the air,
Hail feels like diamonds,
Hail tastes like water.

Kyle Guest (6)
St Gerard's RC Primary School, Castle Vale

Frosty Looks Like A Snowman

Frost feels icy,
Frost sounds like a brick,
Frost looks like a rabbit,
Frost smells like a red nose,
Frost tastes like icy water.

Mexxii Ryan (6)
St Gerard's RC Primary School, Castle Vale

Magic Glitter And Rainbows

I am magical and I have special powers,
I am fluffy and white,
I have pretty eyelashes,
When my hair flutters in the wind, it leaves a trail of glitter,
I have four legs but I can fly,
When my horn is warm, it is the colour of a rainbow,
If I am cold, it is gold,
I look like a horse with wings,
What am I?

Answer: A unicorn.

Daisy Taylor (5)
St Mary's Catholic Primary School, Madeley

My Family

M y mummy is lovely,
Y ellow, green, red and blue are colours we use in crafts.

F un board games are what I play with my dad,
A t bedtime, we read stories,
M ondays we go to Nanny's for tea,
I love spending time with Grandad,
L ittle brother loves playing with me,
Y es, family is great!

Leah Walker (5)
St Mary's Catholic Primary School, Madeley

The Great Fire Of London

In 1666, there was a glimmering fire,
It was in the city of London, and the flames got higher.
It started in Pudding Lane in the bakery,
The wooden house caught fire and people ran away.
Everyone was scared,
Because they were not prepared.

Rowan Simmons (6)
St Mary's Catholic Primary School, Madeley

Pretty Things About Birds

The pretty blackbird has a nice beak,
He has black on him,
He has beautiful patterns on him,
He is a bit greedy.
He eats berries and insects and worms,
Wood pigeons eat seeds and grain,
Crops feed birds,
Woodpeckers eat insects.

Hope Mapenzi Onyango (6)
St Mary's Catholic Primary School, Madeley

The Egg Hunt

He has big ears,
He is cute and fluffy,
He hides chocolate eggs,
He decorates the egg with patterns,
He hops very high,
He has whiskers and a round, fluffy tail,
Who is he?

Answer: *The Easter bunny.*

Billy George Palmer (6)
St Mary's Catholic Primary School, Madeley

The Scary Hairy Monster

A monster feels hairy,
A monster looks big and scary,
A monster tastes like slugs and snails,
A monster smells like stinky tails,
A monster's roar sounds like thunder,
A monster really is a wonder!

Cerys Thomas (5)
St Mary's Catholic Primary School, Madeley

The Dragons

D angerous dragons,
R ed-hot fire,
A s mean as a goblin,
G reen dragons are angry,
O n the castle,
N obody can defeat them,
S cary and horrible.

Samuel Lloyd Carrington (5)
St Mary's Catholic Primary School, Madeley

House On My Back

I might be small, but I have long eyes,
I move slow and am very quiet,
I lick leaves, they taste good,
I am slimy like a slug,
My shell is my home,
What am I?

Reece Fellows (6)

St Mary's Catholic Primary School, Madeley

Free

F ast, hopping, green animal that looks like a bird

R unning to get his dinner

O ver the log, it leaps

G etting a fly to eat.

Jan Samsom (5)
St Mary's Catholic Primary School, Madeley

My Cat

H uge and big, like a planet,
U nder the covers, he sleeps,
G rowls at my little brother,
O n the wall, he scratches.

Harris Moorcroft (5)
St Mary's Catholic Primary School, Madeley

Dino

D inosaurs are stinky and angry,

I can hear them roar,

N oisy and stomping,

O h no, one is knocking on my door!

Isaac Groom (5)

St Mary's Catholic Primary School, Madeley

Ruby

R uby is my bulldog,

U p she jumps on the sofa to snuggle,

B eware of Ruby, she protects me,

Y es, she loves me!

Blaine Fletcher-Cook (5)

St Mary's Catholic Primary School, Madeley

What Am I?

Brown hair with black eyes
Honest and I hate lies
I've travelled a long way
And here now I stay
Arabic was what I spoke
Always clean and chic
I learn English very fast
I will add future to my past
I like to have fun
To learn to jump and run
Who am I?

Omar Bilal Alfreahat (7)
St Mary's CE Primary School, Shawbury

Octopus

O range skin,

C atches fish,

T entacles that are wavy,

O ctopuses have eight tentacles,

P uts fish in its big mouth,

U nstoppable suckers,

S uper strong suckers.

James Ireland (7)
St Mary's CE Primary School, Shawbury

Octopus

O range and red skin,
C amouflaged body,
T entacles long,
O pen eyes watching,
P uffy, big head,
U p and up he goes,
S trong suckers.

Noah Willoughby (6)
St Mary's CE Primary School, Shawbury

Whale

W ater is blue and wavy,

H appily swimming along,

A big, happy whale,

L onely, big whale,

E yes are big.

Evalyn Durie (6)

St Mary's CE Primary School, Shawbury

Shark

S harp, shiny teeth,
H unting for food,
A lways hungry,
R eally fast swimmer,
K ing of the sea.

Peter Williams (6)
St Mary's CE Primary School, Shawbury

Shark

S harp teeth,

H ungry,

A lways hungry,

R eally fast in the sea,

K ing of the sharks.

Harry Williams (6)
St Mary's CE Primary School, Shawbury

Shark

S harp teeth,
H appily swimming along,
A ngry shark,
R ude and naughty,
K ills fish.

James Dale (7)
St Mary's CE Primary School, Shawbury

Whale

W avy water,

H appily swimming along,

A big whale,

L ong, big whale,

E yes are big.

Isabelle Knight (7)
St Mary's CE Primary School, Shawbury

Shark

S harp teeth,
H unting for food,
A ngry shark,
R ude and scary,
K ing of the sea.

Harleigh May Jones (6)
St Mary's CE Primary School, Shawbury

Shark

S harp teeth,
H unting for fish,
A lways hungry,
R eally huge,
K ing of the sea.

Luukas Dean (6)
St Mary's CE Primary School, Shawbury

Shark

S harp teeth,
H ungry shark,
A ngry shark,
R ude and naughty,
K illing fish.

Alfie Titley (7)
St Mary's CE Primary School, Shawbury

Fish

F ast at swimming,
I nteresting shapes and sizes,
S hiny and slow,
H uge and colourful.

Mollie Oakley (6)
St Mary's CE Primary School, Shawbury

Fish

I have small fins,
I have a small body,
I like to eat coral,
What am I?

Answer: A fish.

Abigail Beckett (6)

St Mary's CE Primary School, Shawbury

What Am I?

I have eight thin, long tentacles,
I have an invisible mouth,
I like to eat crabs and shrimp,
What am I?

Jake Hanson (6)
St Mary's CE Primary School, Shawbury

Shark

S caly sharp,
H unting for fish,
A ngry,
R ude,
K ing of the sea.

Joshua Poole (6)
St Mary's CE Primary School, Shawbury

What Am I?

I have eight long tentacles,
I have a big, wobbly body,
I like swimming slowly around,
What am I?

Eva Marie Buckley (6)
St Mary's CE Primary School, Shawbury

Shark

S parkly teeth,

H appy,

A ngry,

R ude,

K ing of the sea.

Frayer Evans (6)

St Mary's CE Primary School, Shawbury

What Am I?

I have eight long tentacles,
I have a big, bushy head,
I like to swim around,
What am I?

Ellie Giatsios (7)
St Mary's CE Primary School, Shawbury

What Am I?

I have long tentacles,
I have lots of suckers on each tentacle,
I like fish,
What am I?

Mia Edmonds (6)
St Mary's CE Primary School, Shawbury

What Am I?

I have a small, scaly body,
I have very small eyes,
I like colourful coral,
What am I?

Chloe Williams (7)
St Mary's CE Primary School, Shawbury

What Am I?

I have shiny scales,
I have a little body,
I like to eat colourful coral,
What am I?

Jessica Butler (6)
St Mary's CE Primary School, Shawbury

What Am I?

I have razor-sharp teeth,
I have a long, smooth body,
I like to eat fish,
What am I?

Ethan Green (6)
St Mary's CE Primary School, Shawbury

What Am I?

I have long, sharp teeth,
I have little beady eyes,
I like to eat fish,
What am I?

Charlie Lowe (6)
St Mary's CE Primary School, Shawbury

What Am I?

I have short, splashy fins,
I have small eyes,
I like to eat coral,
What am I?

Nahla Lewis (7)
St Mary's CE Primary School, Shawbury

What Am I?

I have sharp teeth,
I have a smooth body,
I like to eat fish,
What am I?

Summer Williamson (6)
St Mary's CE Primary School, Shawbury

Messing With A Princess

My hair is black.
It's hurting my back.
My hair is long.
Let me sing a song.
I have a friend.
Who helps me to mend.
He is a boy.
Who never acts like a toy.
I have a pet.
Who never wants to get wet.
My pet is a tiger.
But it seems he is on fire.
Same as the colour of his fur.
My other friend has no shoe.
He is stuck like glue.
His colour is blue.
And he always gives clues.

Elle Lyza Marie Makinano Mananquil (7)

Tiverton Junior And Infant School, Selly Oak

Circle Of Love

Mummy and Daddy love hugs and kisses,
They love me lots and give me best wishes.
When I was one, I had just begun,
When I was two, I was nearly new,
When I was three, I was hardly me.
When I was four, I was not much more,
When I was five, I was just alive,
But now I am six and I am clever,
So I think I'll be six forever.

Shyanne Rahman (6)
Tiverton Junior And Infant School, Selly Oak

A Furry Pet

I have long, pointy ears,
I'm the prey of humans, foxes and bears.
I wear a furry coat,
My legs are fast but short.
I live in a hole,
My neighbour is a mole.
My home is very muddy,
But I am very cuddly.
My favourite food is carrots,
But I am not a parrot.
What am I?

Answer: A rabbit.

Mohammed Kaif Ali (7)
Tiverton Junior And Infant School, Selly Oak

Arctic Foxes

A rctic foxes search for their prey at night
with very good sight,

R acing after animals which won't stay still,

C old climate,

T ired after a long chase, but at last, they
catch something,

I cy cold, shivering cold, until you're...

C osy at home with a penguin liver.

Nirel Wangui Shitseswa (6)

Tiverton Junior And Infant School, Selly Oak

Cunning Crocodile

C unning smiles I will show,

R un away from me,

O r I might eat you in a bite,

C rocodile tears you might shed,

O pening my huge mouth,

D angerous like a dinosaur,

I am a fierce predator,

L ooking for prey,

E very trick I will play.

Ryan Damdam (7)

Tiverton Junior And Infant School, Selly Oak

In Outer Space

I have always wanted to go to space,
See the sparkly stars all around me.
I would fly like a shooting star,
Seeing all the planets from above.
I could step on the moon,
And watch the sun from afar,
Until it was time to go back to Earth,
It would be so much fun in outer space.

Zaina Amrane (6)

Tiverton Junior And Infant School, Selly Oak

All About Desserts

Desserts look like chocolate cocoa cream,
Desserts sound like a yummy treat,
Desserts smell like a yummy flavour
shooting through the air,
Desserts feel like heaven that we can never
bear,
Desserts taste like golden syrup sitting on
your tongue,
But my favourite is pancakes!

Assiyah Rassam (7)

Tiverton Junior And Infant School, Selly Oak

The Glowing Snow

On my lawn, there was so much snow,
I could not stand its glow.
I had a lawn to mow,
but couldn't go because of the snow.
It was so bright,
We had a snow fight.
It was a great sight
In the end, we all hugged tight.

Amal Sameed (6)
Tiverton Junior And Infant School, Selly Oak

At School

S eeing my friends five days a week,
C aring about others,
H onest about everything that I do,
O nly try my best,
O h, I hope I get things right,
L earning things I haven't done before.

Eloise Hope (6)
Tiverton Junior And Infant School, Selly Oak

Summer Fun

Summer looks like the sun on the sand,
Summer sounds like waves in the sea,
Summer feels like feet on hot sand,
Summer smells like barbecues sizzling,
Summer tastes like cold, chilly ice cream,
Summer is all about fun.

Anna Housaini (7)
Tiverton Junior And Infant School, Selly Oak

My Dad

B aba, is what I call him.

A lways joking, laughing and playing.

B adminton is what he likes best.

A dmiring me, loving me, hugging me.

Shahan Hamzah Ashraf (6)

Tiverton Junior And Infant School, Selly Oak

Young Writers Information

We hope you have enjoyed reading this book – and that you will continue to in the coming years.

If you're a young writer who enjoys reading and creative writing, or the parent of an enthusiastic poet or story writer, do visit our website **www.youngwriters.co.uk**. Here you will find free competitions, workshops and games, as well as recommended reads, a poetry glossary and our blog.

If you would like to order further copies of this book, or any of our other titles, then please give us a call or visit **www.youngwriters.co.uk**.

Young Writers
Remus House
Coltsfoot Drive
Peterborough
PE2 9BF
(01733) 890066
info@youngwriters.co.uk

 @YoungWritersUK  @YoungWritersCW